UNITED STATES

CANADA

JAMAICA

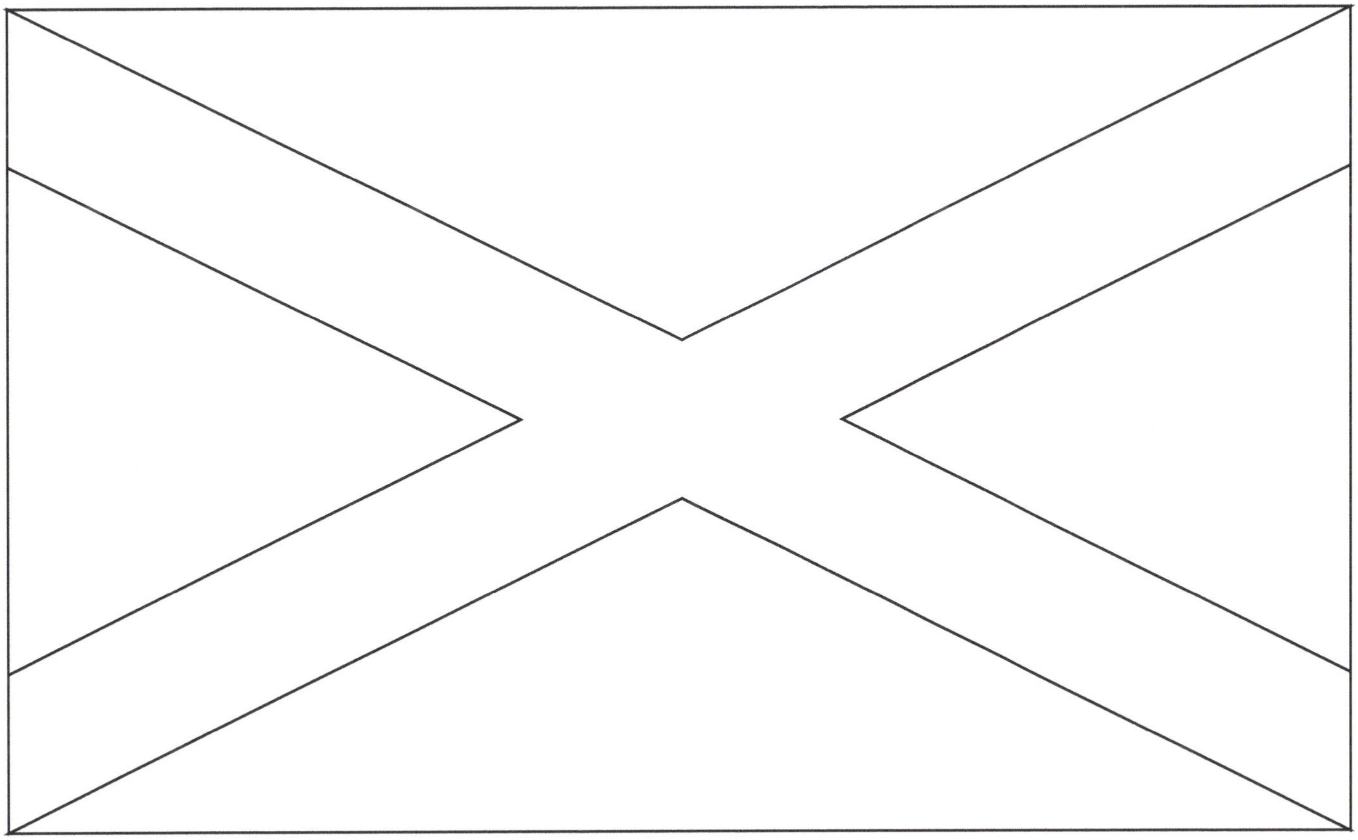

MEXICO

CUBA

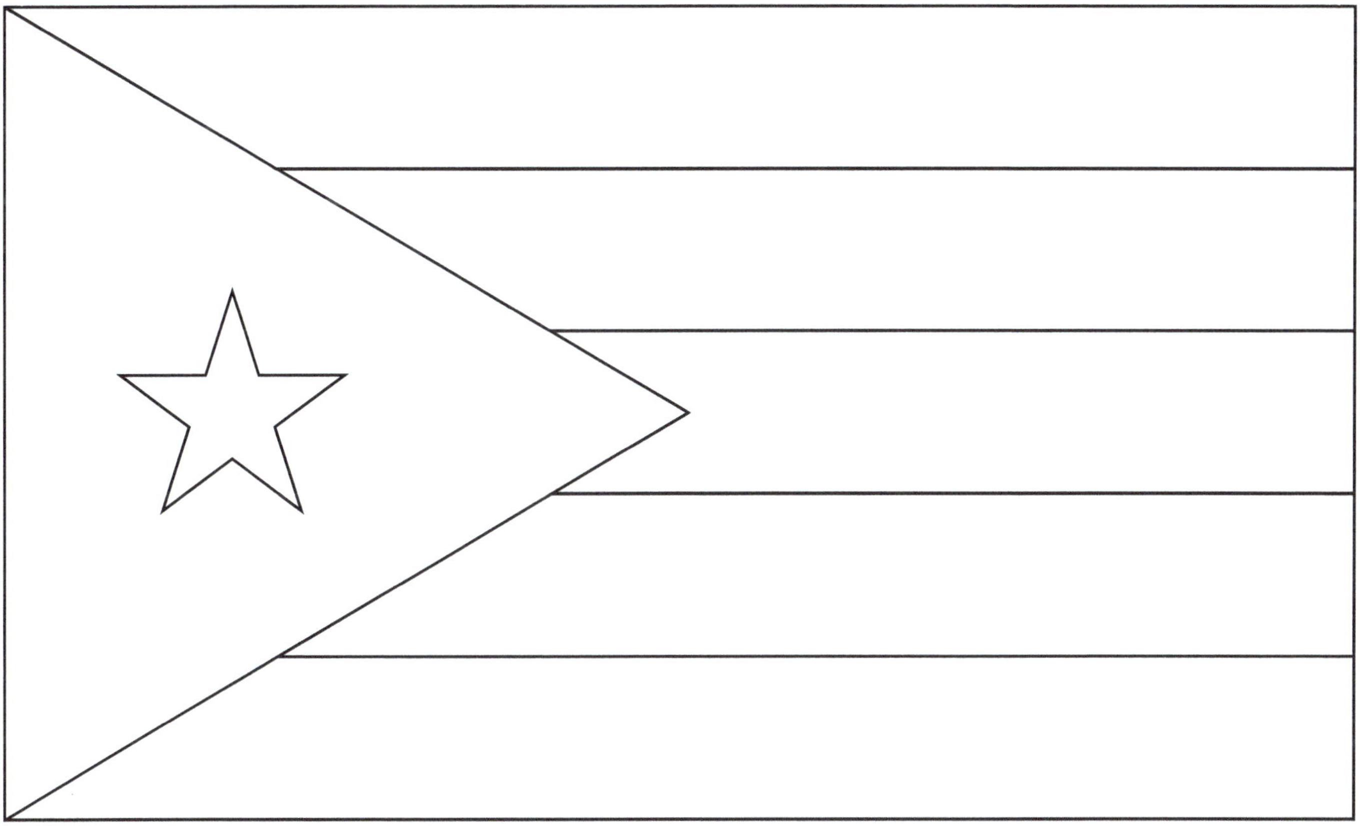

DOMINICA

ANTIGUA AND BARBUDA

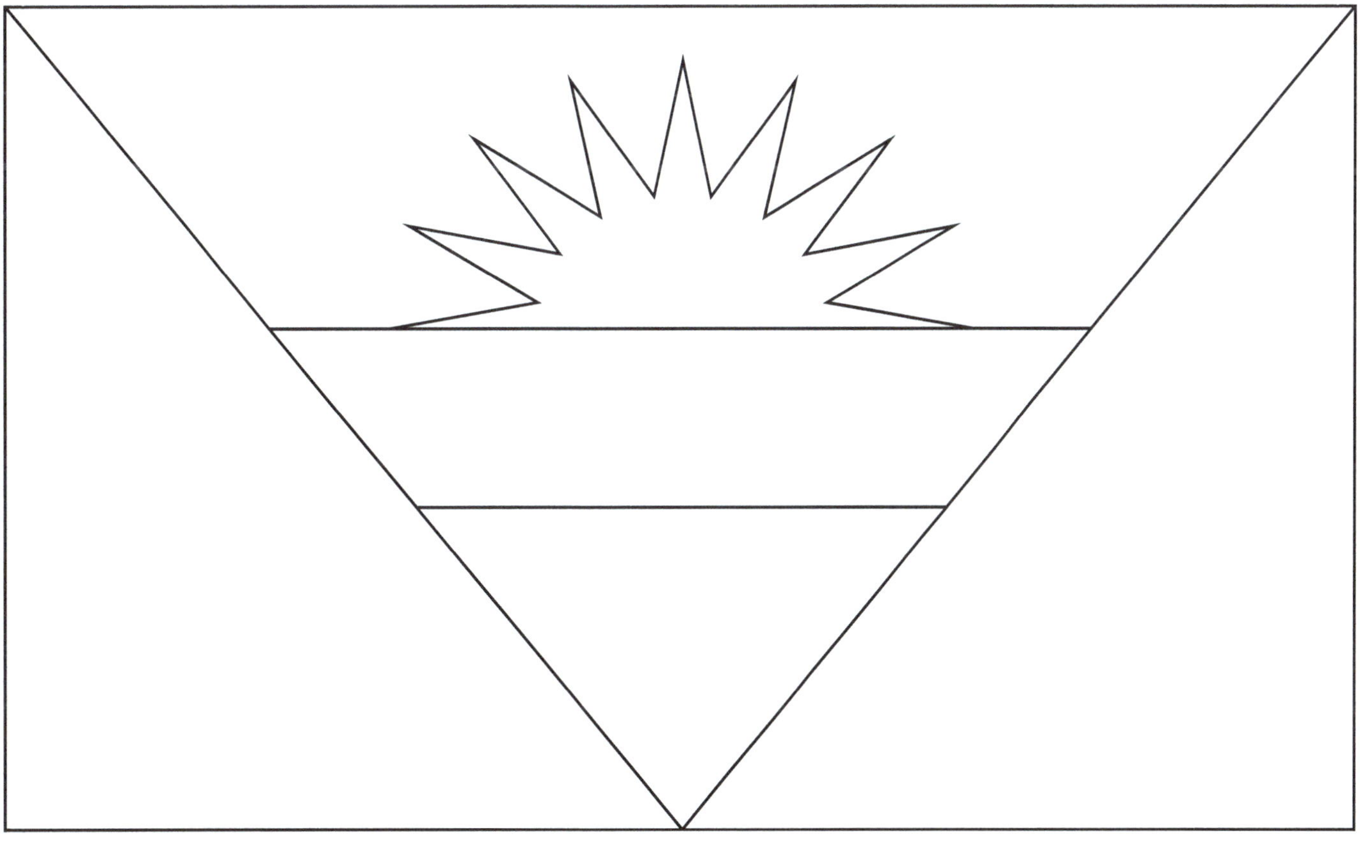

BAHAMAS

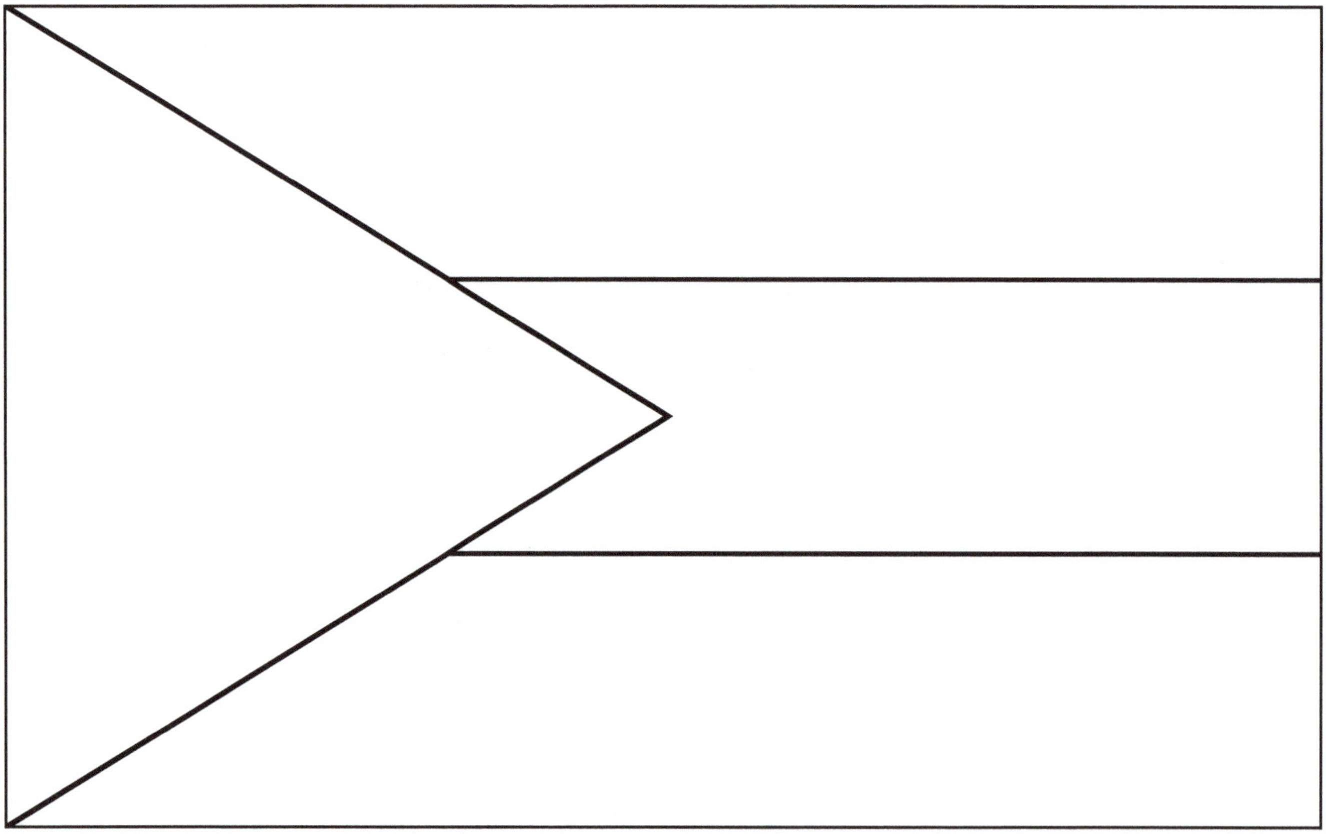

BARBADOS

TRINIDAD AND TOBAGO

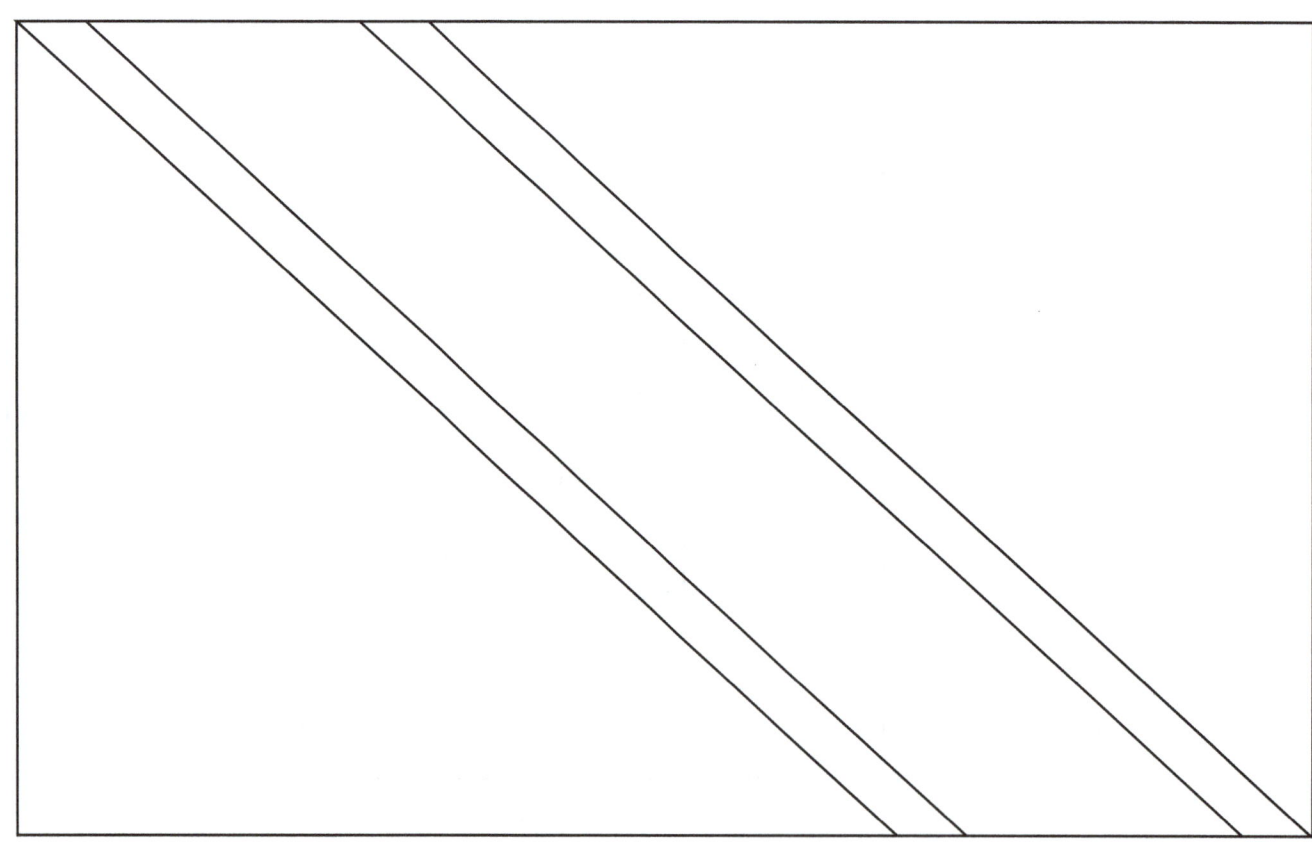

NICARAGUA

COSTA RICA

GRENADA

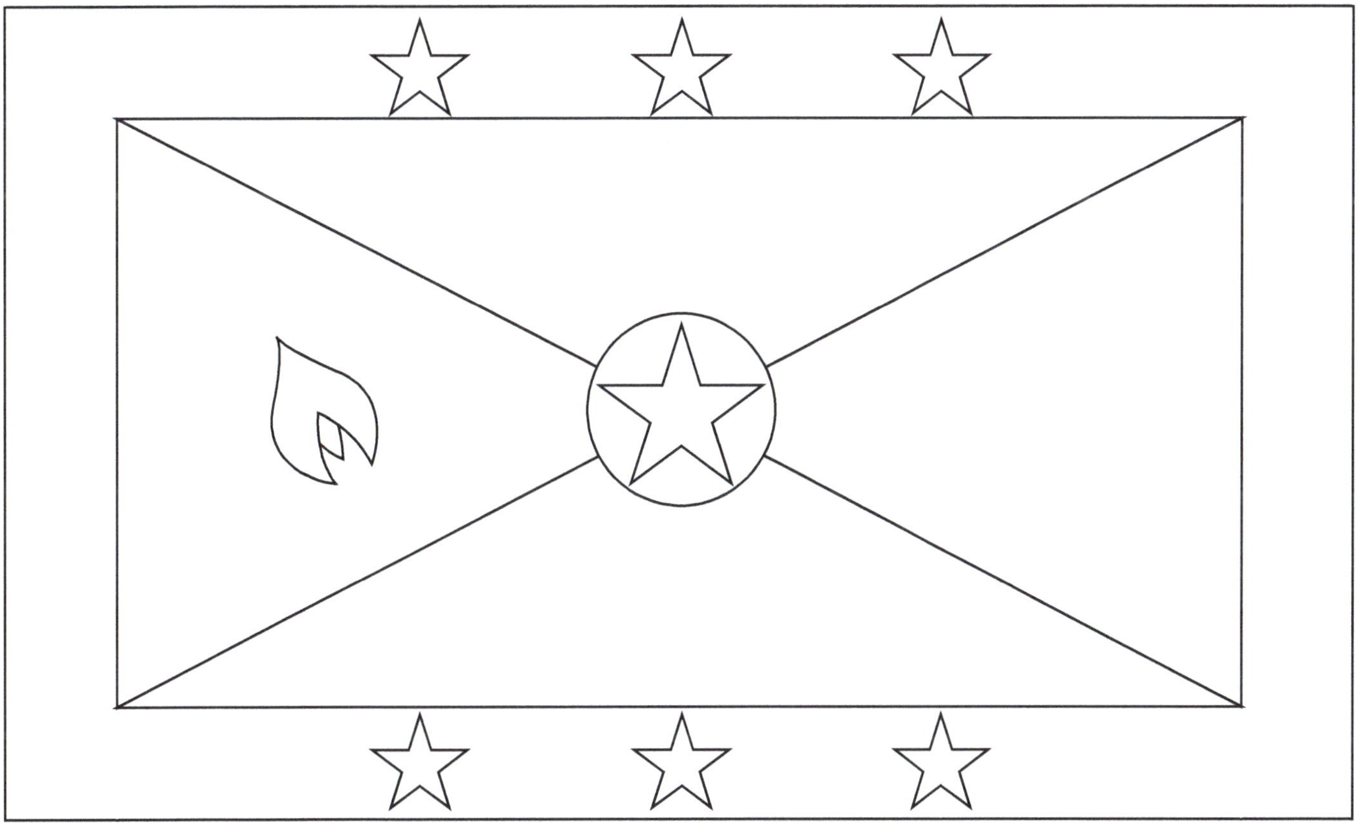

GREENLAND

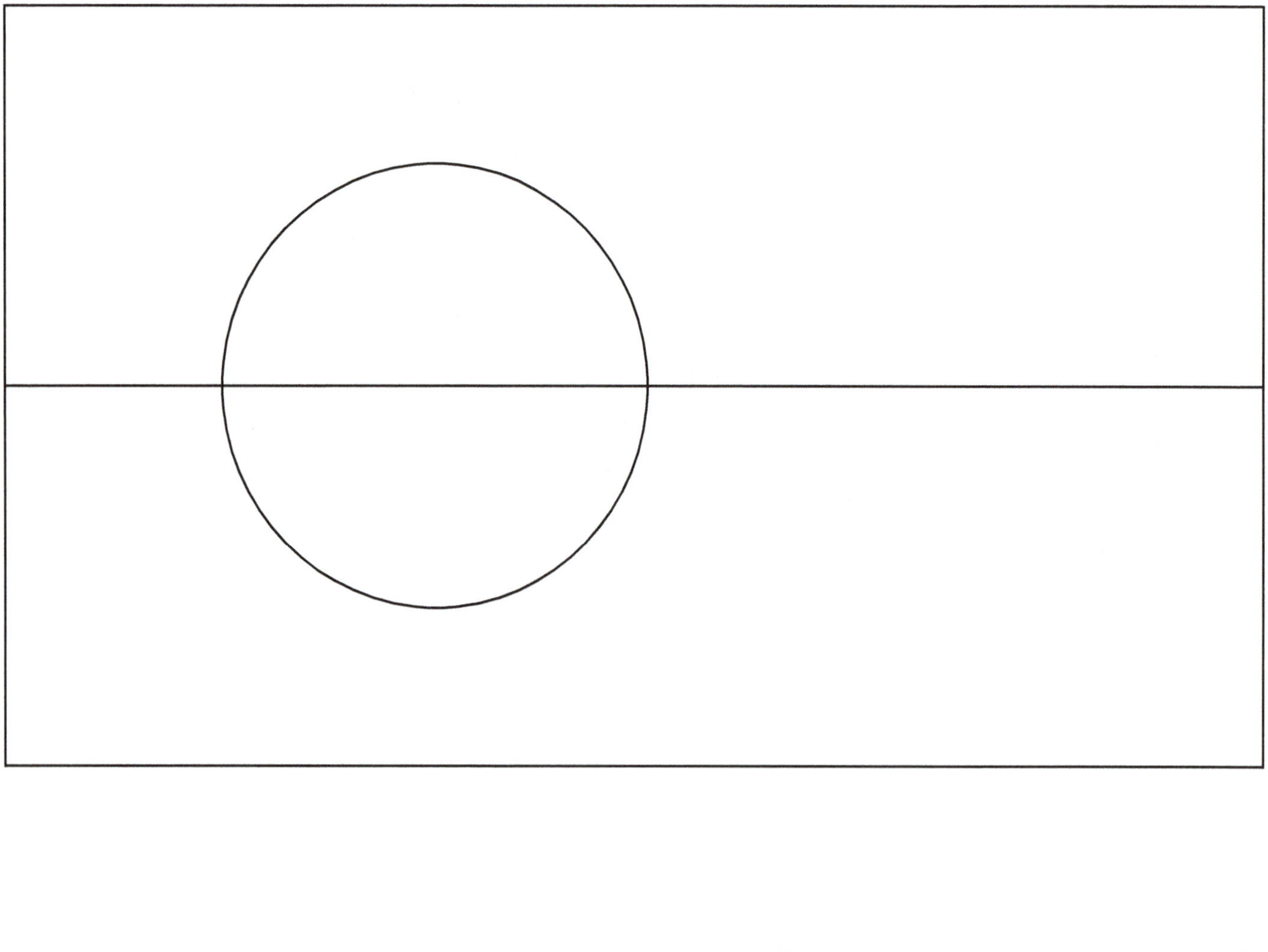

GUATEMALA

HAITI

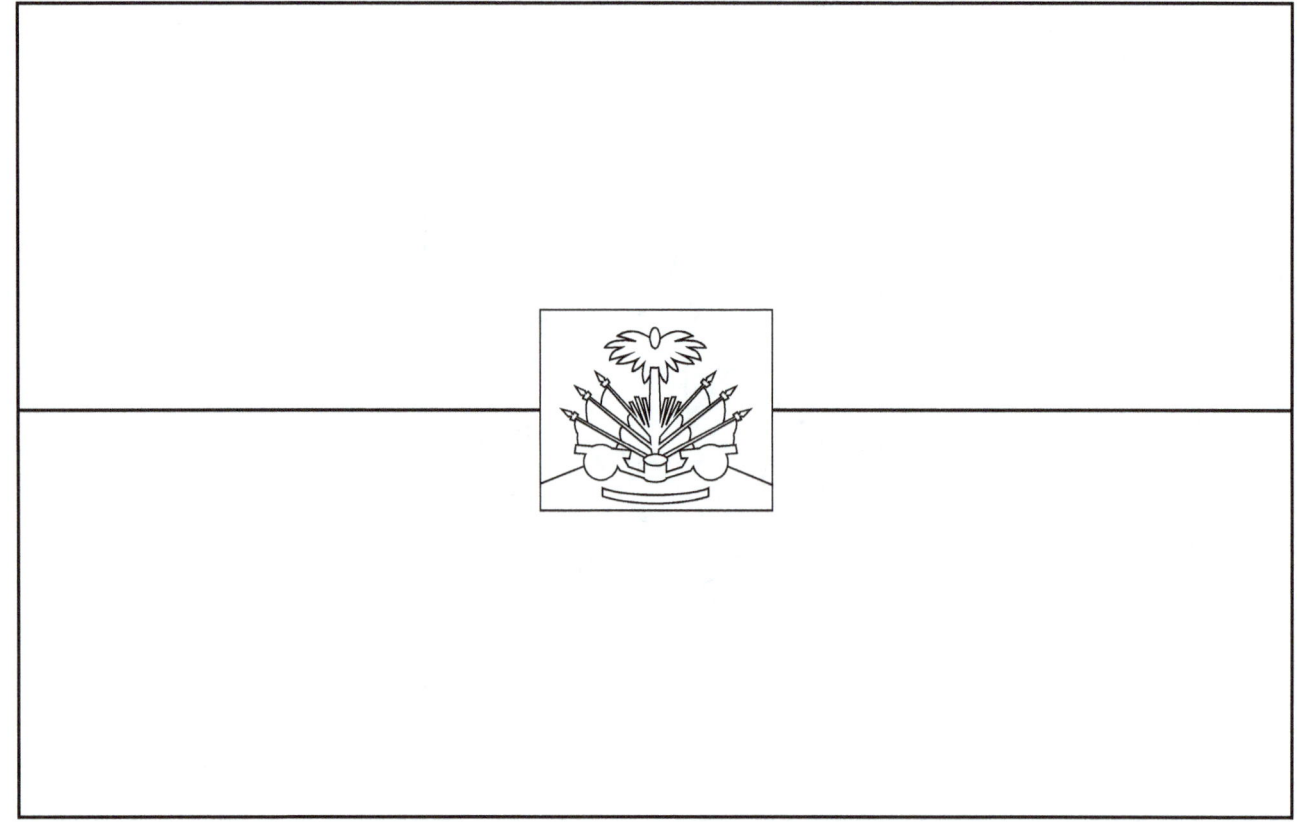

HONDURAS

PANAMA

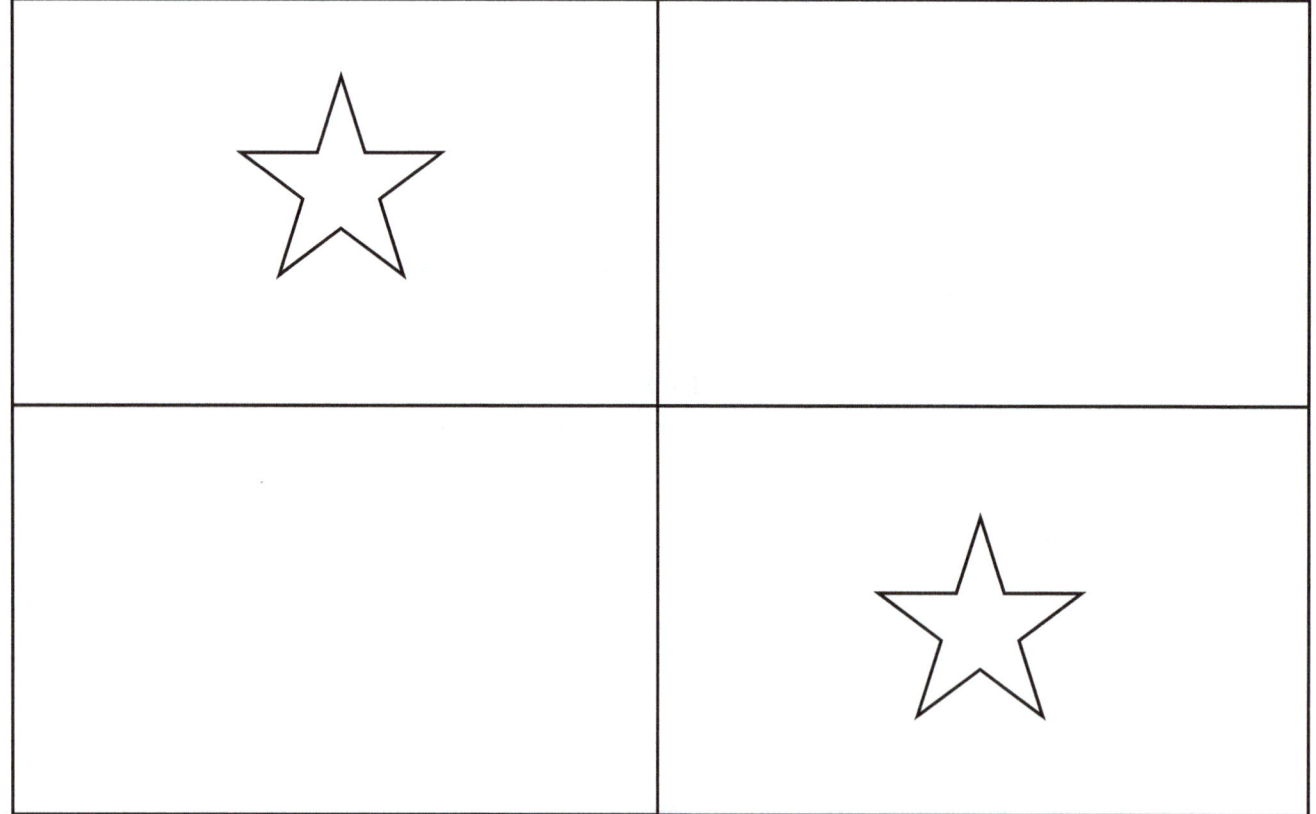

SAINT LUCIA

SAINT KITTS AND NEVIS

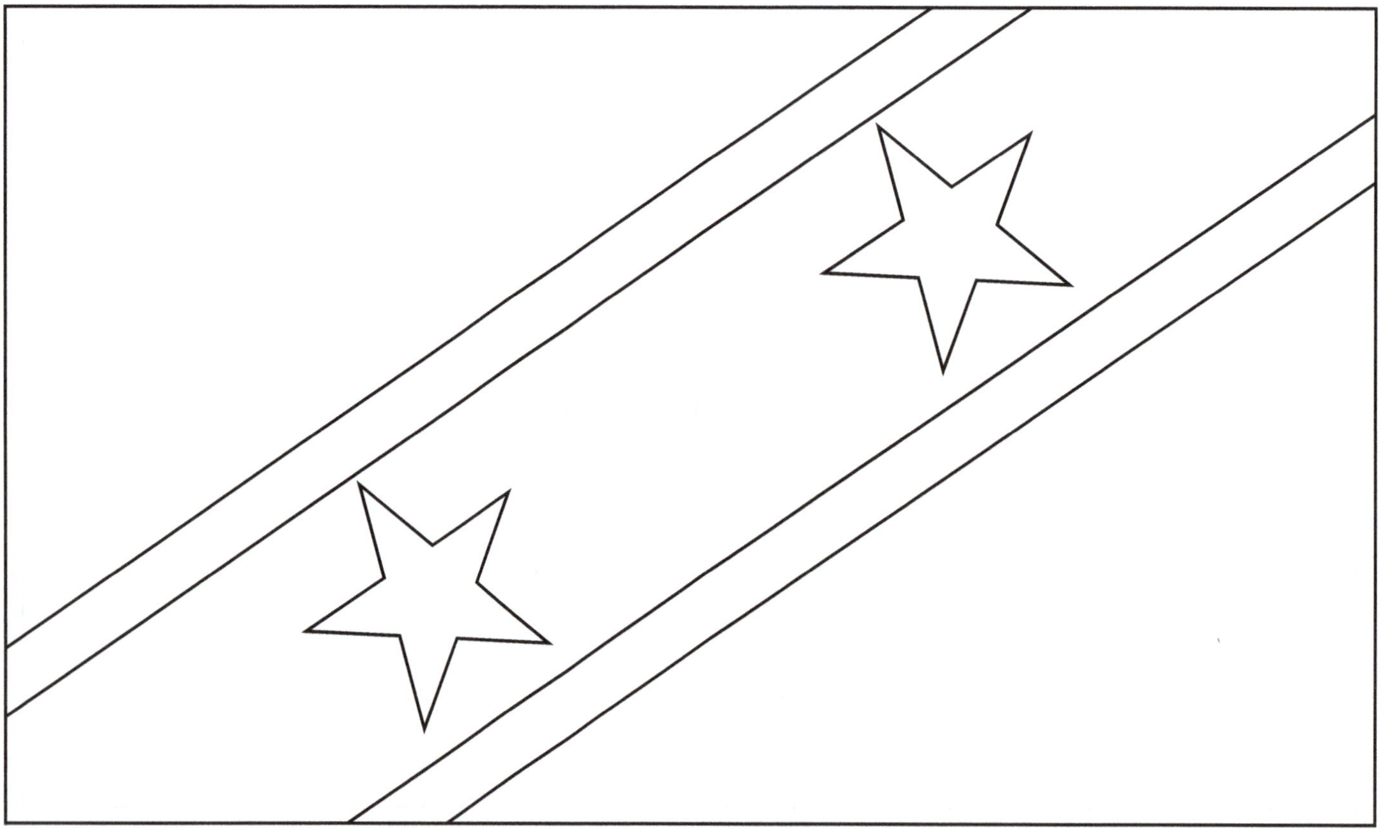

DOMINICAN REPUBLIC

SAINT VINCENT AND THE GRENADINES

PUERTO RICO

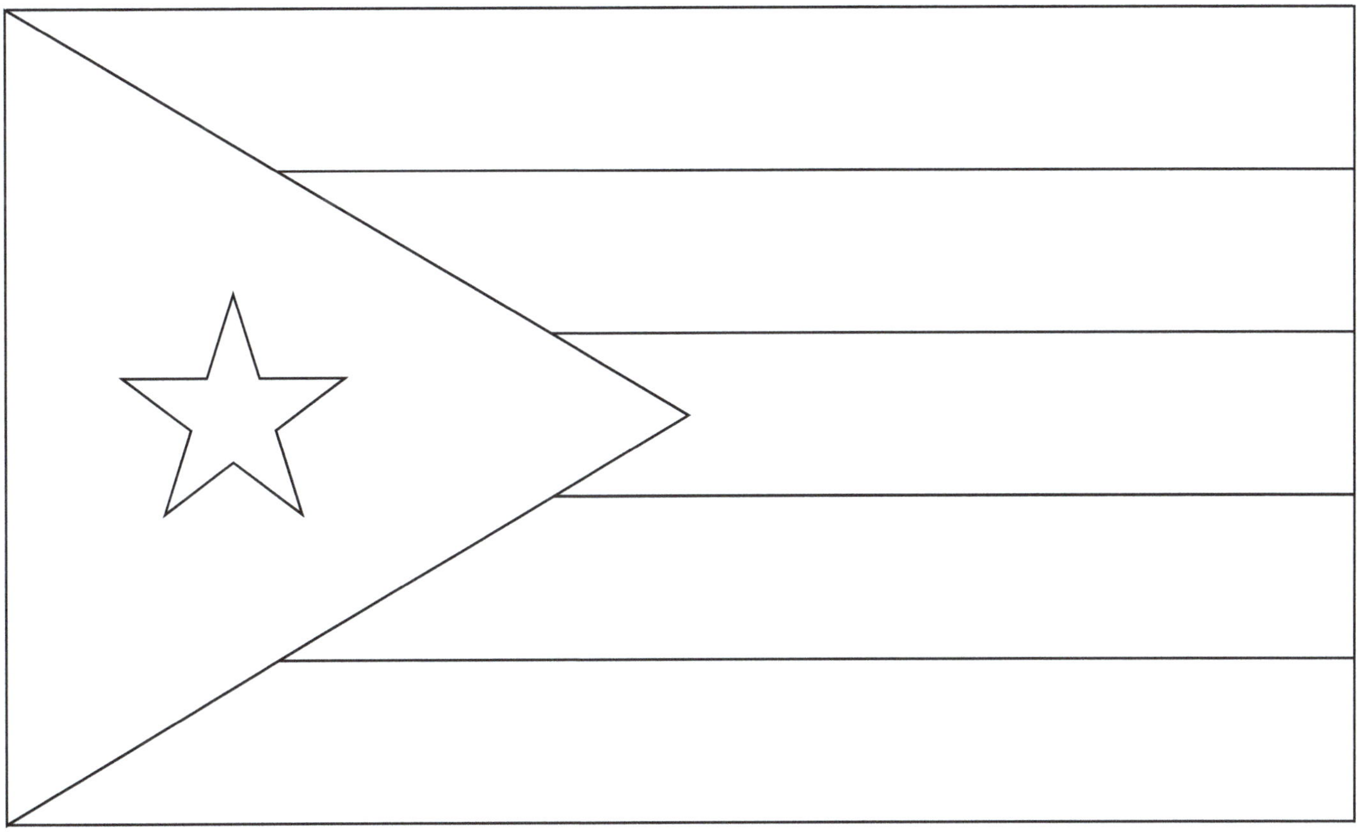

EL SALVADOR

ARGENTINA

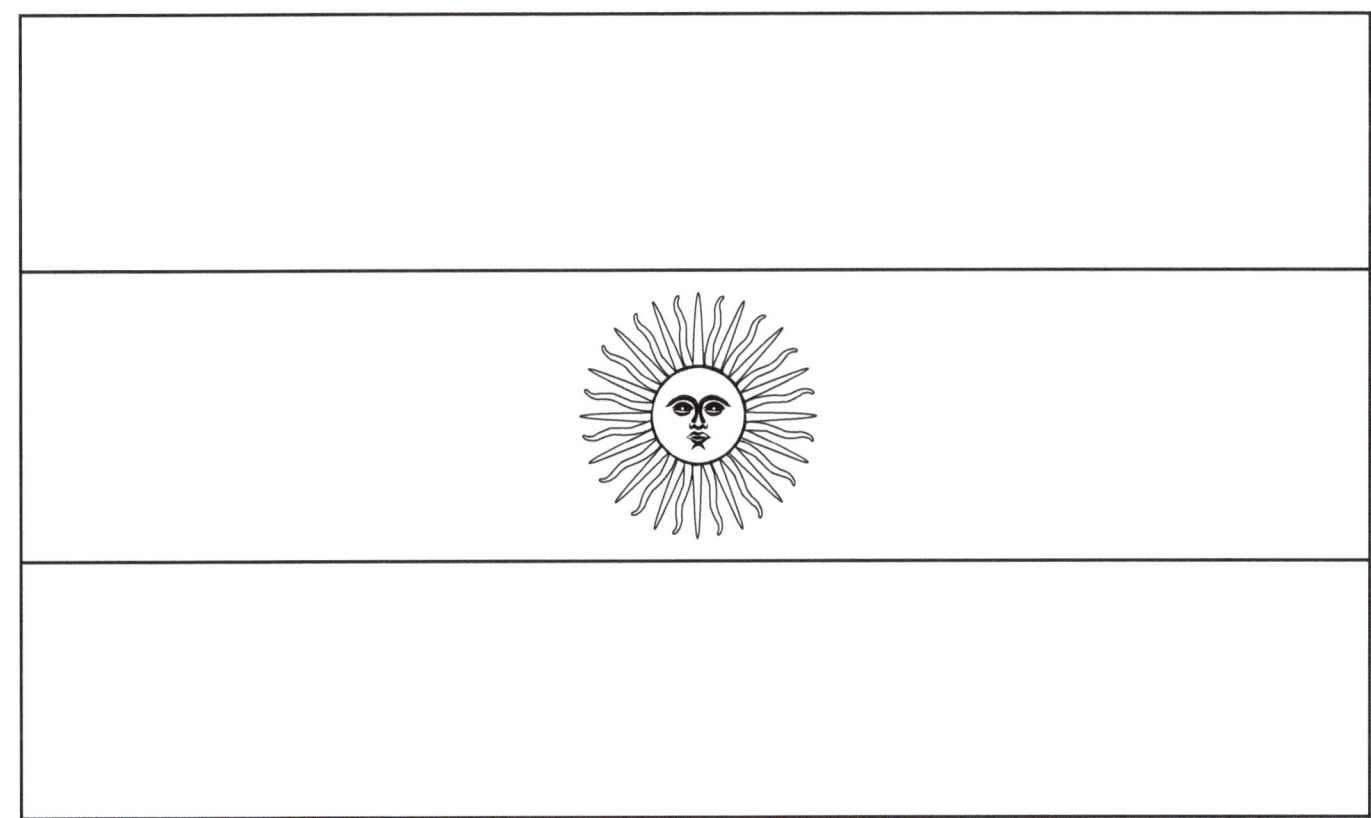

BRAZIL

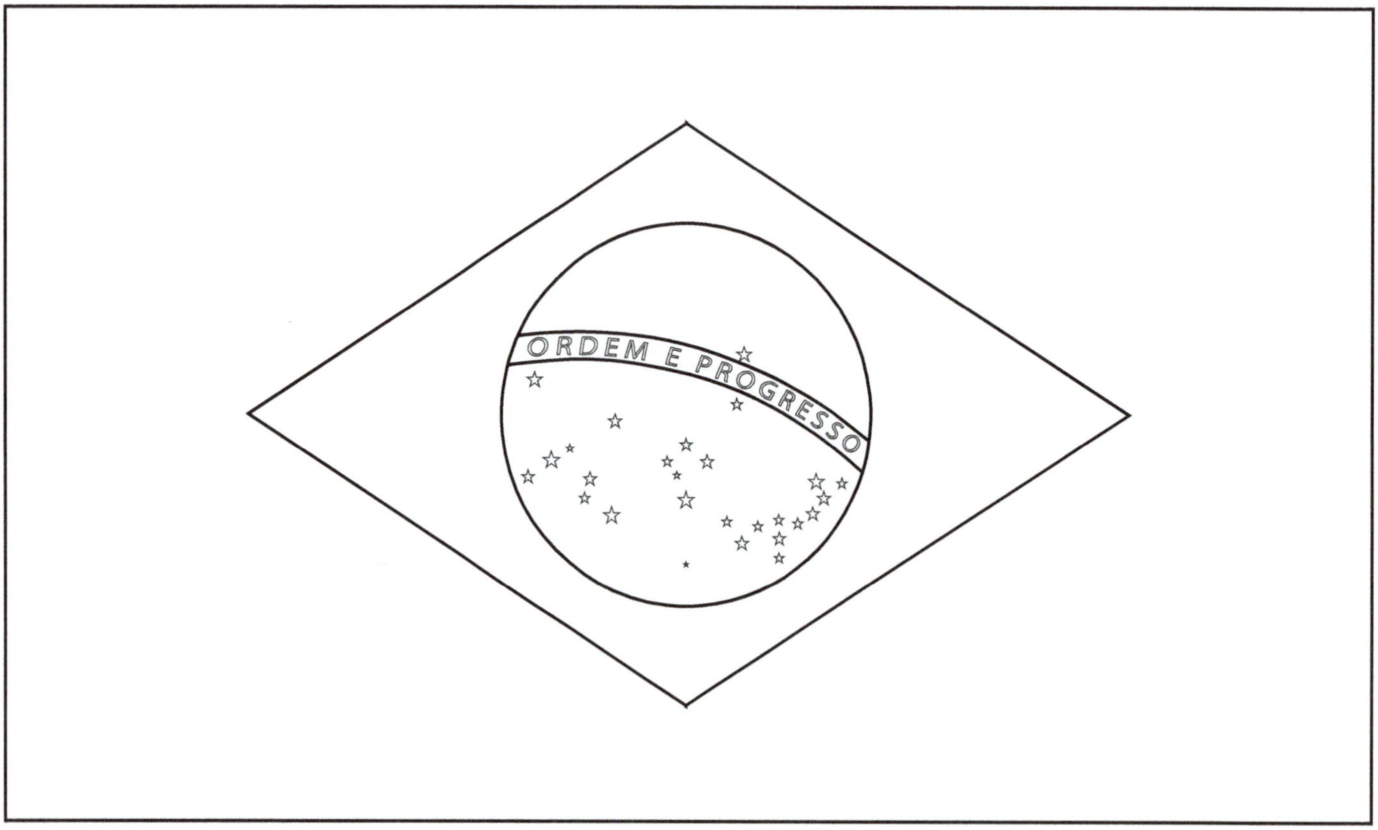

PARAGUAY

BOLOVIA

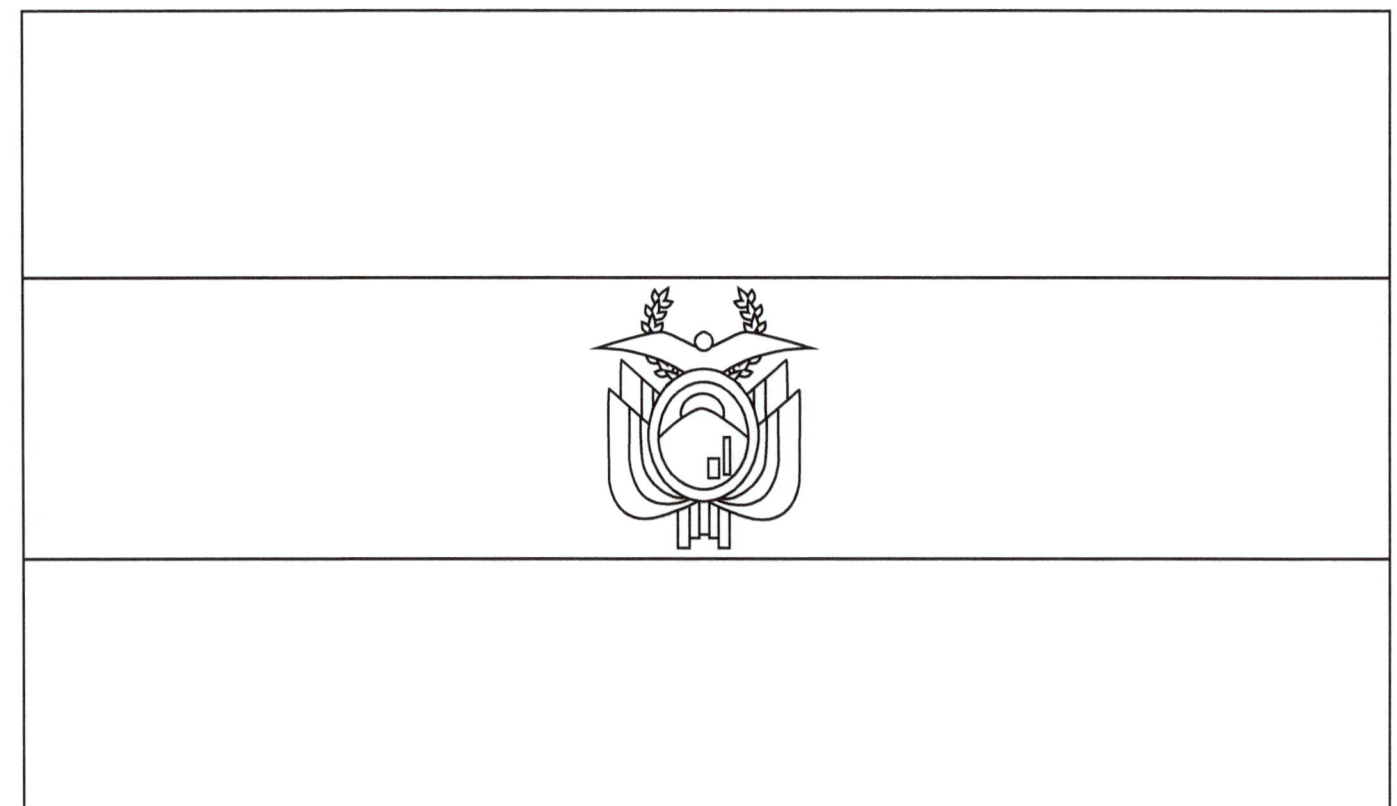

URUGUAY

ECUADOR

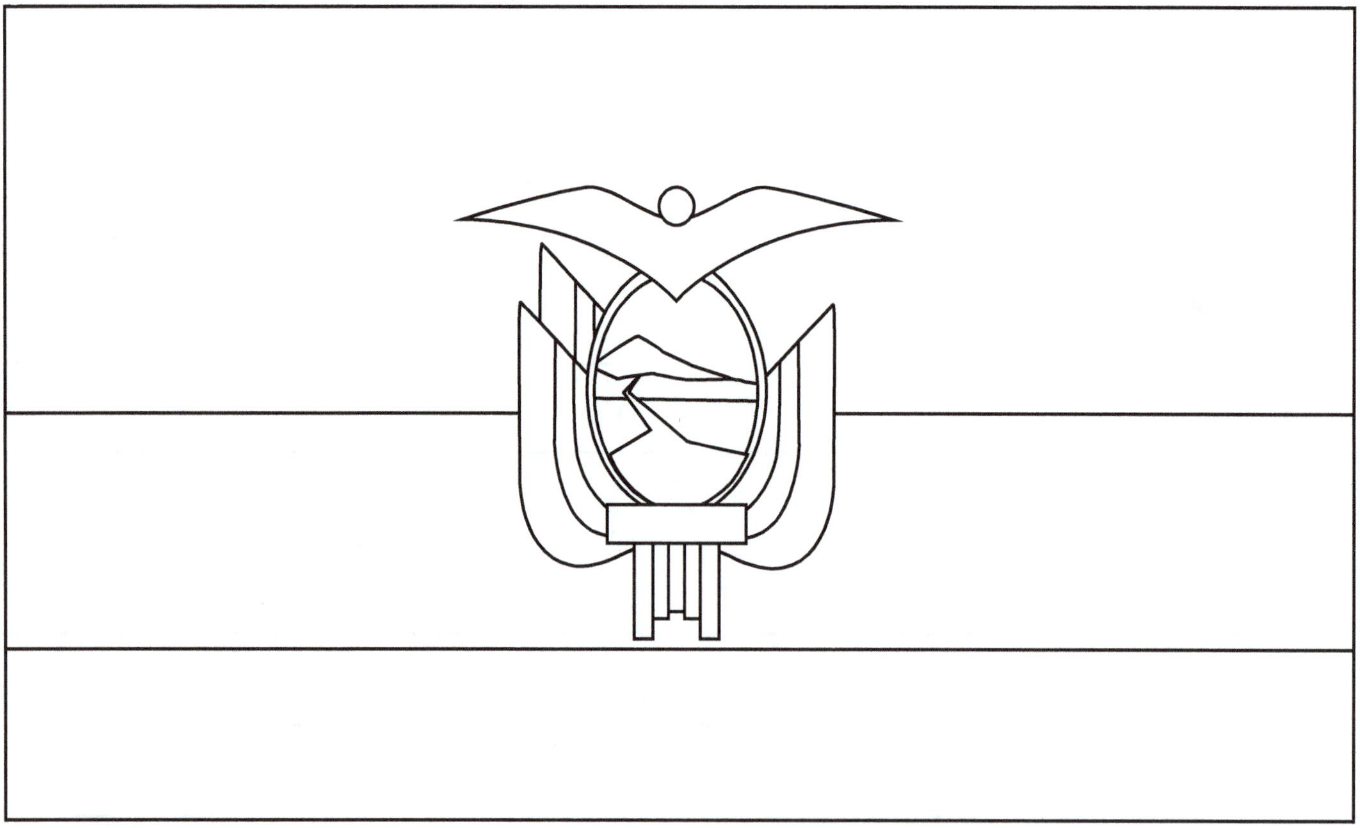

COLOMBIA

PERU

CHILE

VENEZUELA

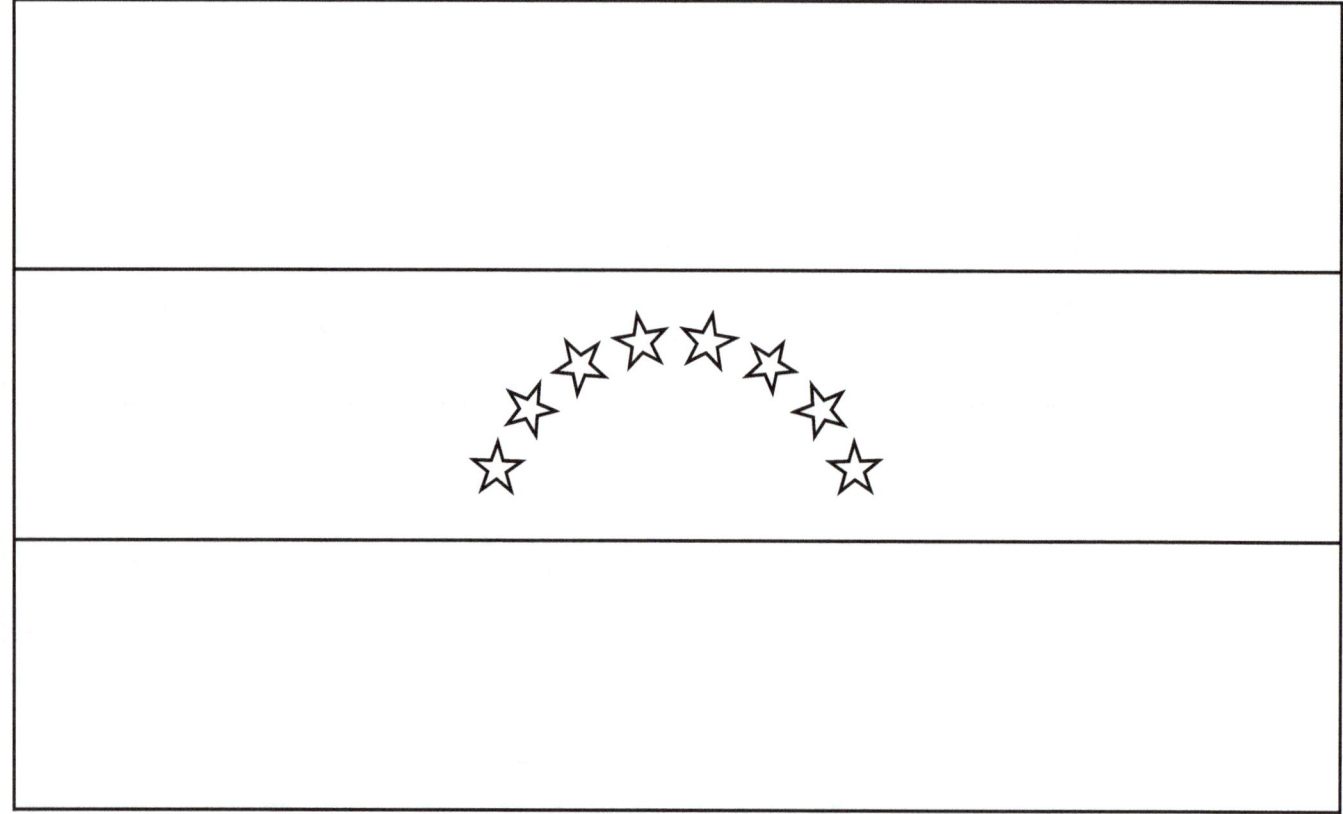

AUSTRALIA

SAMOA

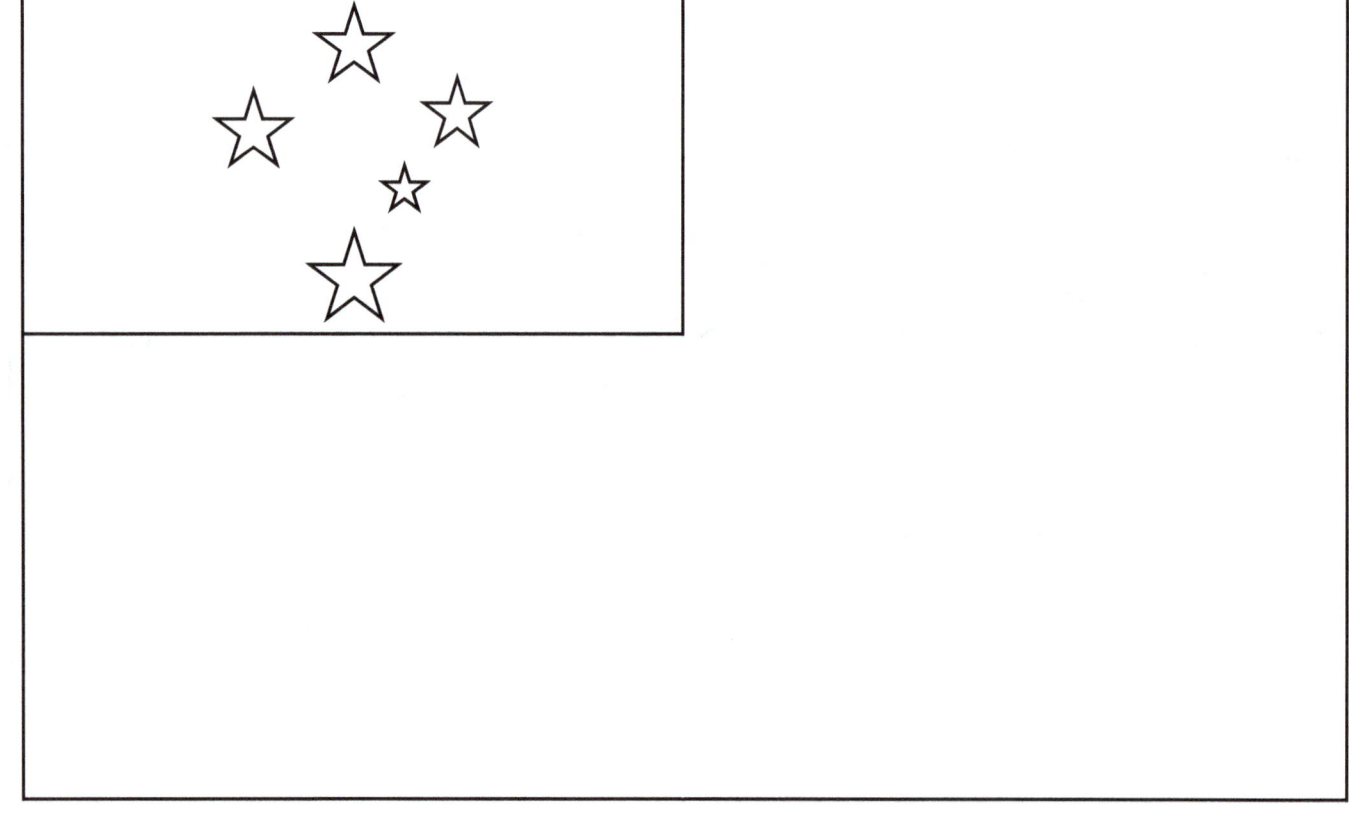

KIRIBATI

SOLOMON ISLANDS

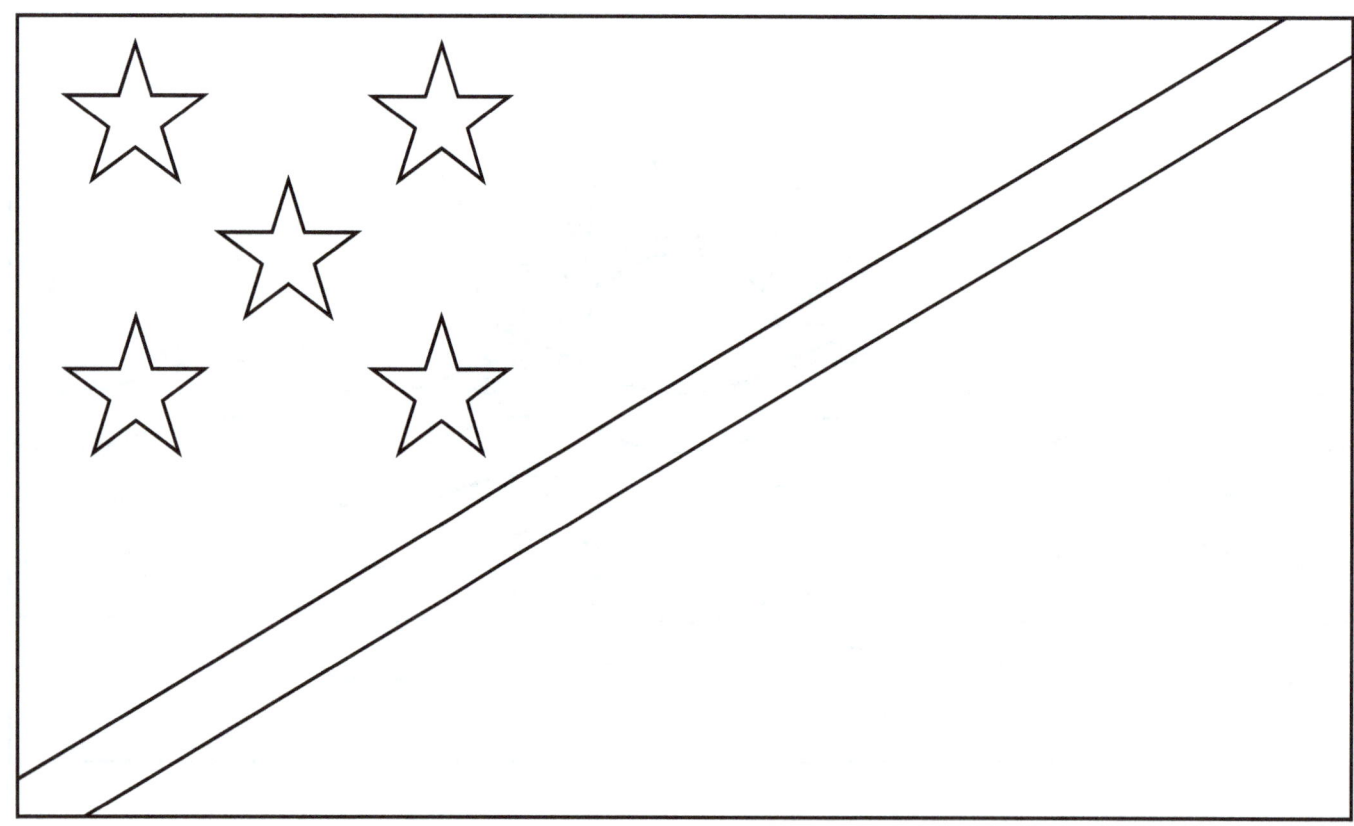

MARSHALL ISLANDS

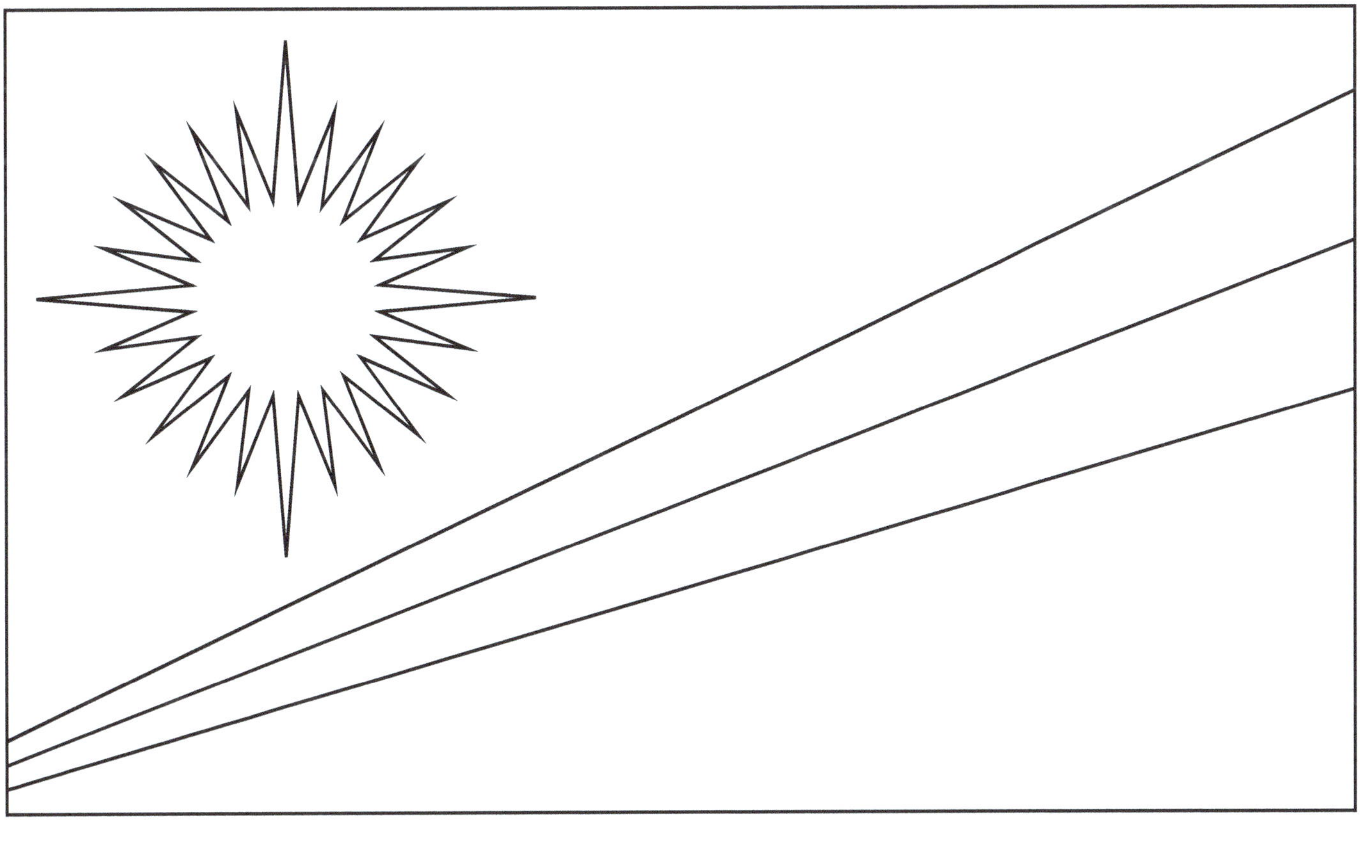

MICRONESIA

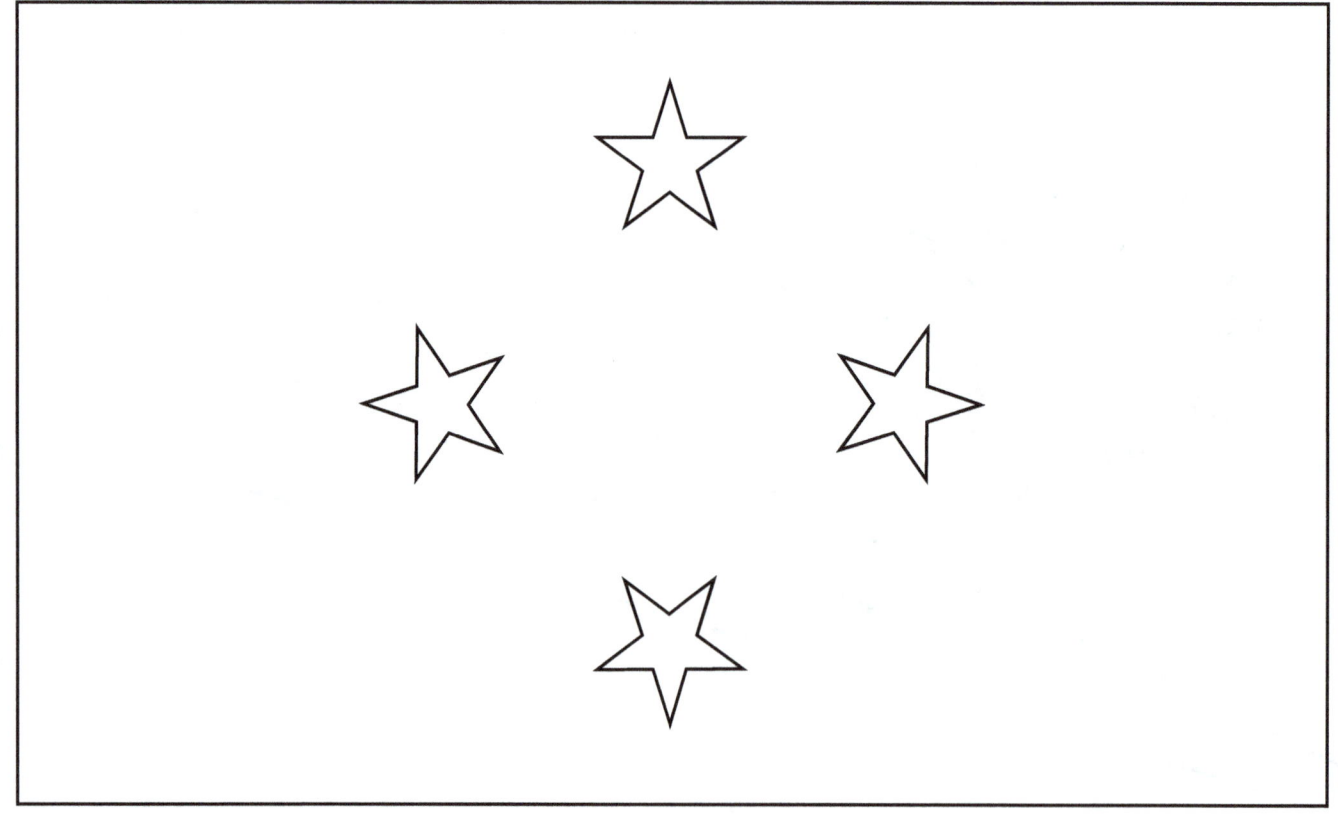

VANUATU

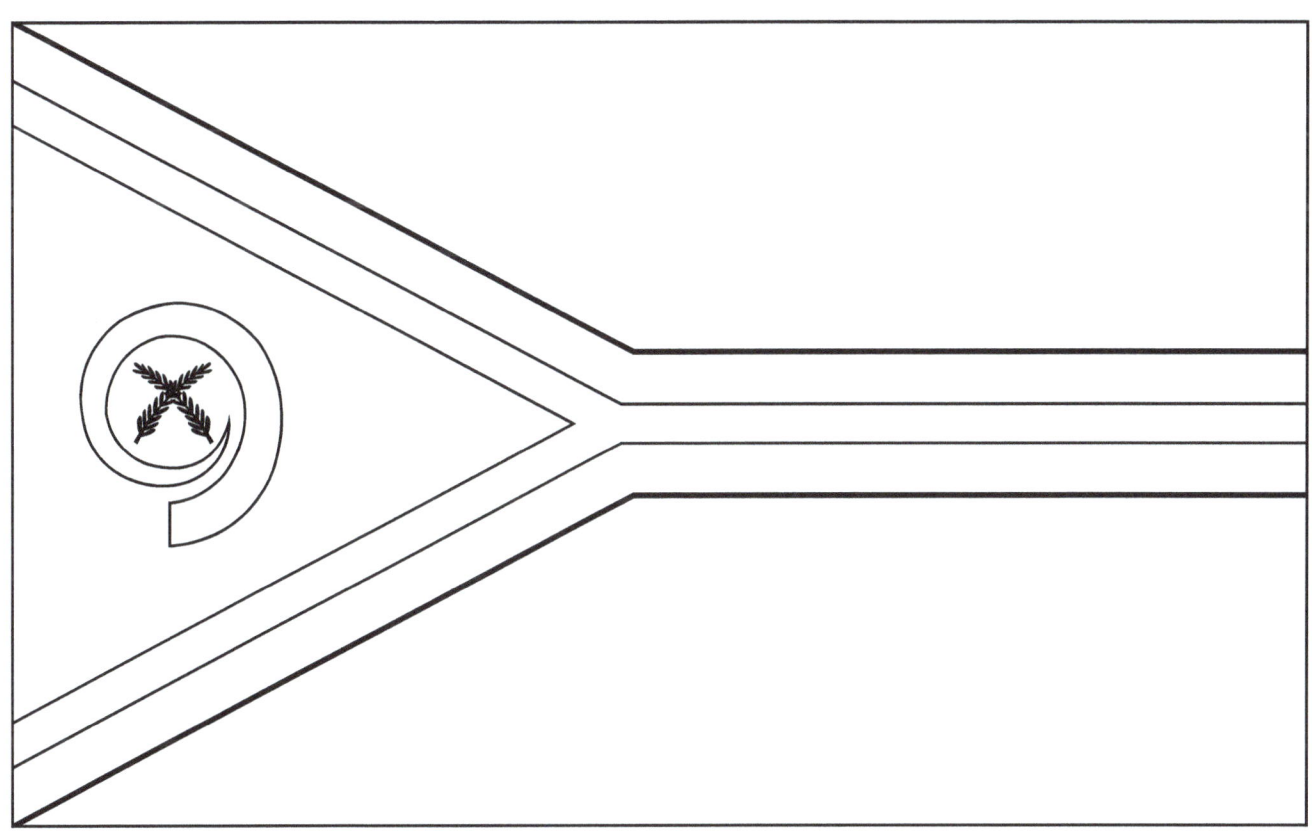

NEW ZEALAND

PALAU

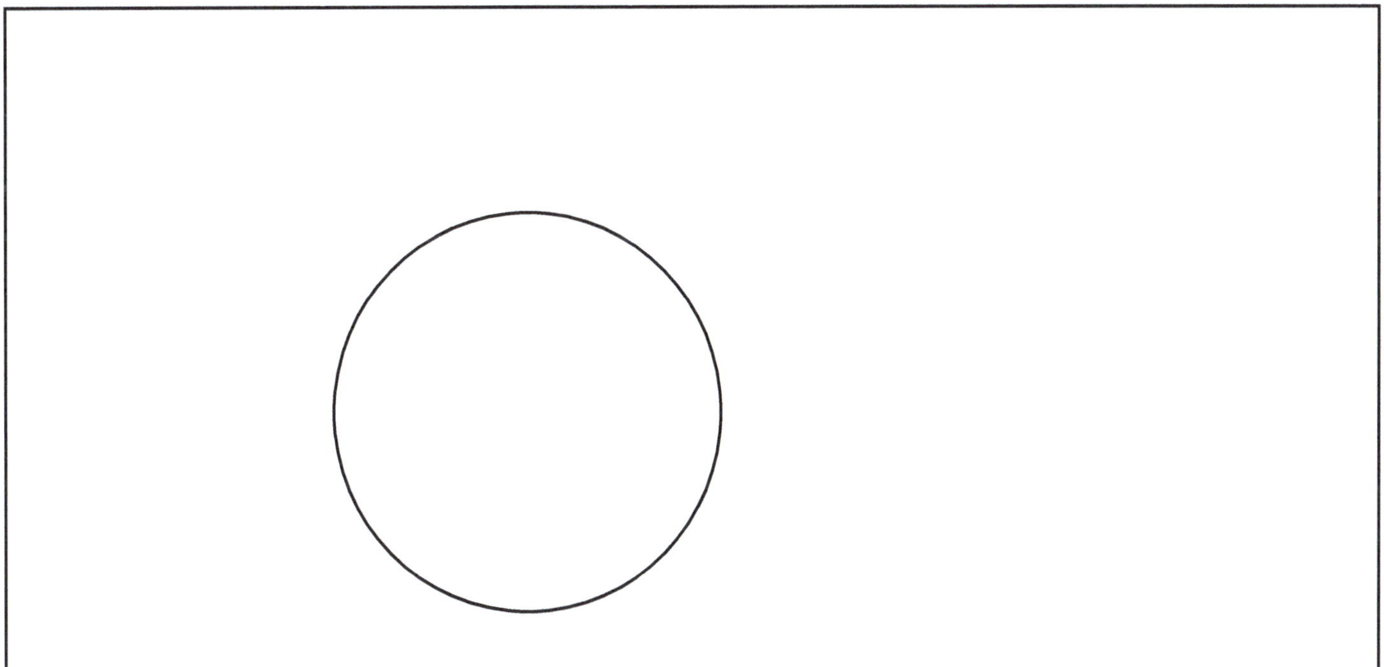

NAURU

PAPUA NEW GUINEA

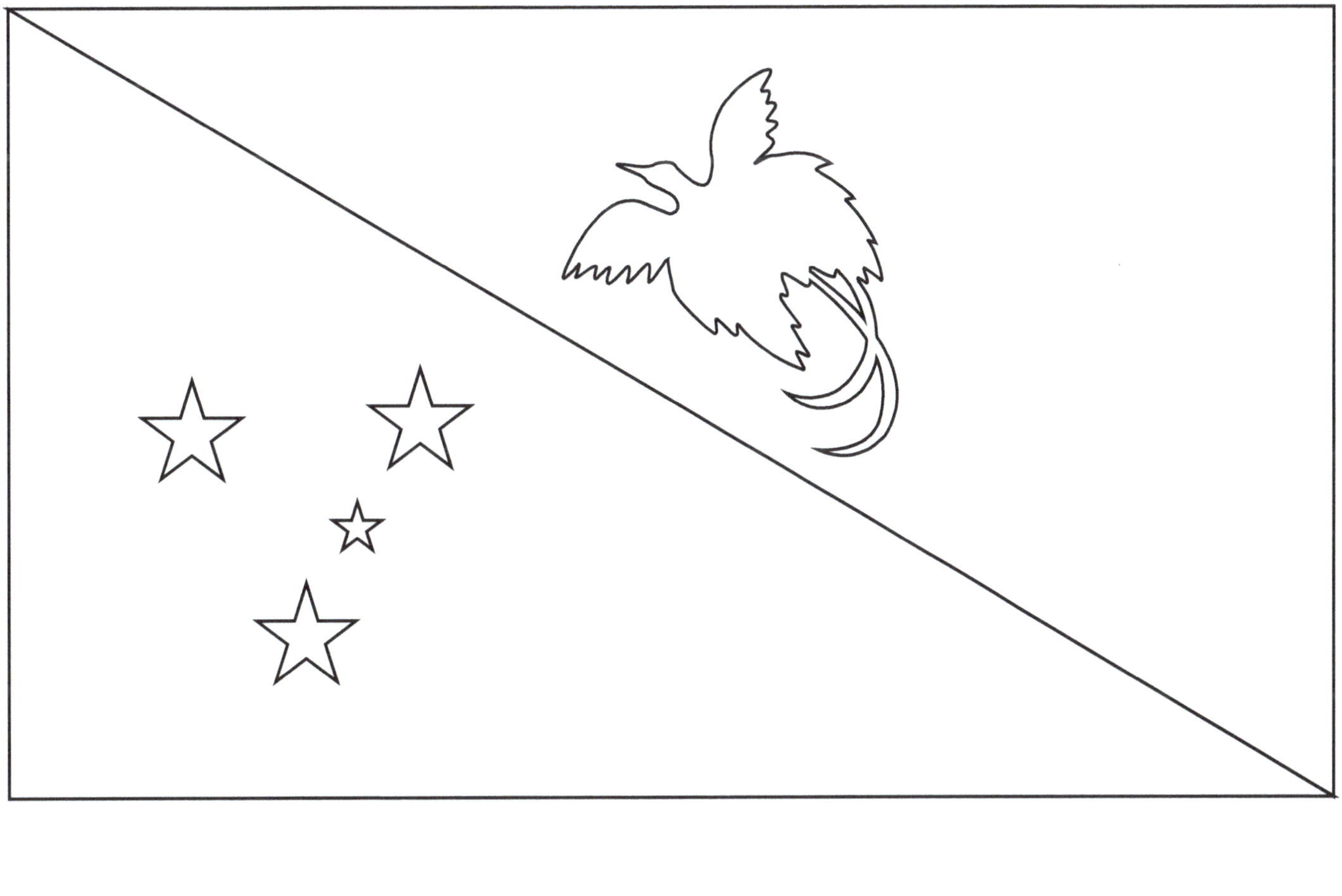

FIJI

TUVALU

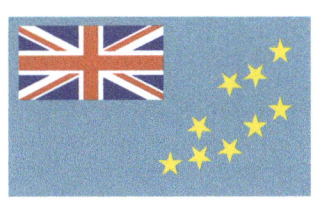

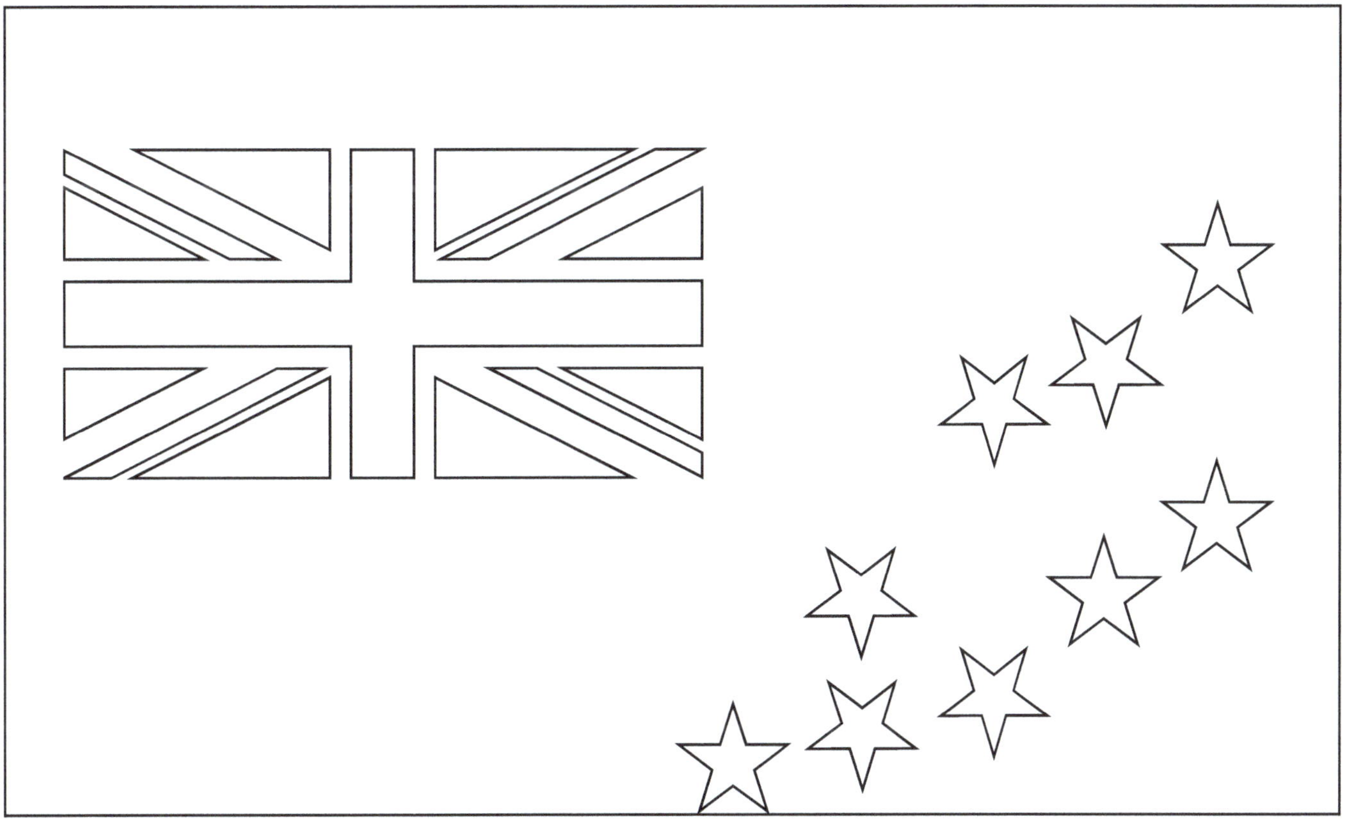

TONGA

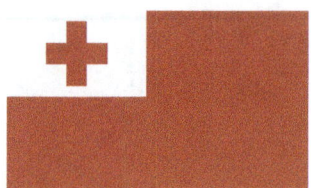

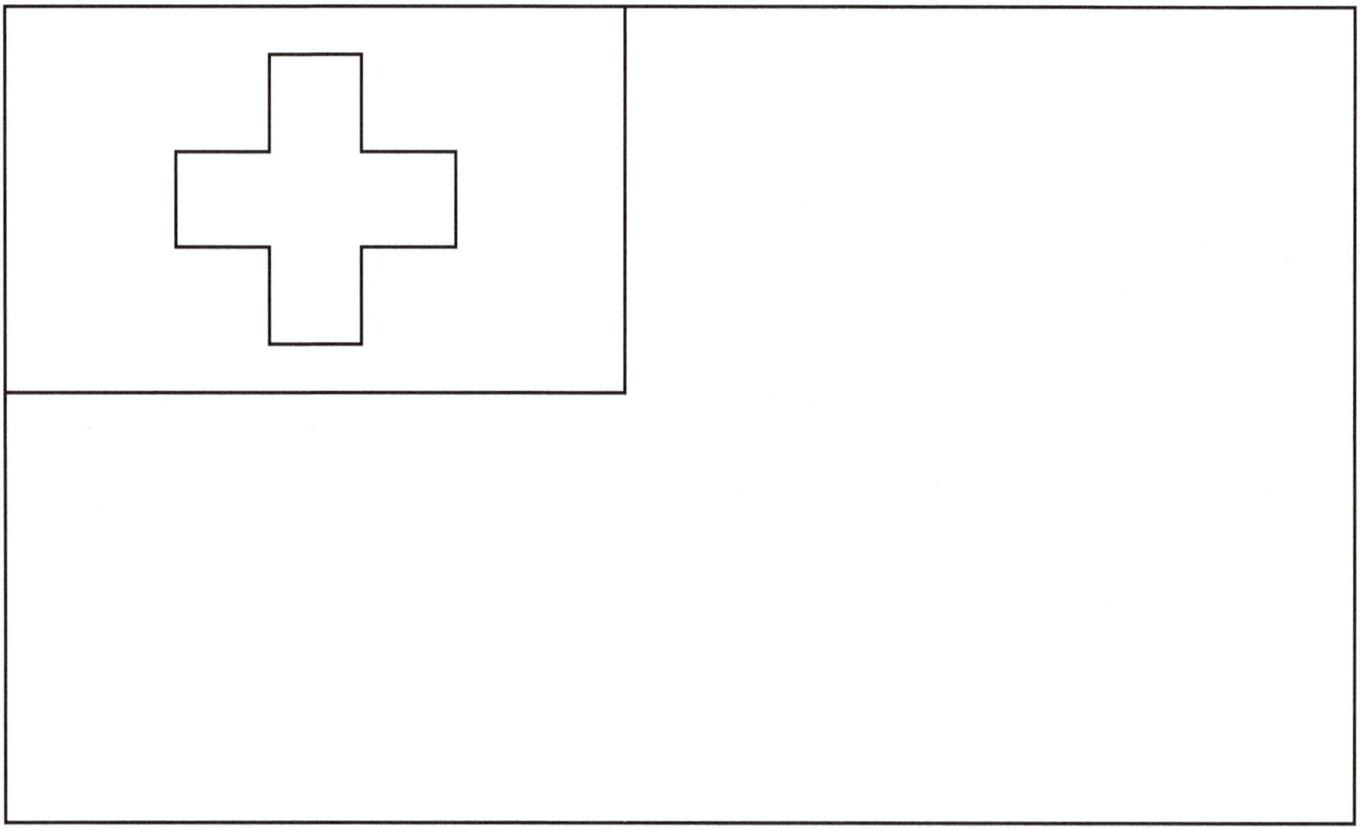